TO

Carol

FROM

Linda

DATE

01 - 03 - 10

Please remember: "You are loved and appreciated"!

Prayers *of* Comfort *for* Those Who Hurt

Hope Lyda

Paintings by
Annie LaPoint

HARVEST HOUSE PUBLISHERS
EUGENE, OREGON

Prayers of Comfort for Those Who Hurt

Text Copyright © 2005 by Hope Lyda.
Text previously appeared in *One-Minute Prayers for Those Who Hurt.*

Artwork Copyright © by Annie LaPoint

Published by Harvest House Publishers
Eugene, Oregon 97402
www.harvesthousepublishers.com

ISBN 978-0-7369-2562-4

All artwork is copyrighted by Annie LaPoint. License granted by Penny Lane Publishing, Inc.® For more information regarding artwork featured in this book, please contact Penny Lane Publishing at info@pennylanepublishing.com.

Design and production by Koechel Peterson & Associates, Inc., Minneapolis, Minnesota

Scripture quotations are taken from the HOLY BIBLE, NEW INTERNATIONAL VERSION®. NIV®. Copyright©1973, 1978, 1984 by the International Bible Society. Used by permission of Zondervan. All rights reserved.

Printed in China

09 10 11 12 13 14 15 / LP / 10 9 8 7 6 5 4 3 2 1

table of contents

MENDING

After the Fall

The bows of the warriors are broken, but those who stumbled are armed with strength.

1 SAMUEL 2:4

Lord, You have made the weak strong. Your power rushes through my veins as I struggle to stand and face the fight of my trial. There are many mighty warriors about me who seem to manage their way fine. But I have taken a fall. All that I have worked hard for crumbles to the ground.

Yet, I also know what it is like to fall into Your strength—to surrender my will to Your own, to know that there is a good thing taking shape that I cannot see right now. You cover me with strength and ability. You will carry me through the days ahead.

Healing the Break

You will say then, "Branches were broken off so that I could be grafted in." Granted. But they were broken off because of unbelief, and you stand by faith. Do not be arrogant, but be afraid.

ROMANS 11:19-20

I make room for You in the most indirect ways. Instead of inviting You into my life, Lord, and asking You to rule over it with Your love and mercy, I force the situation. I fail, I stumble, I break off branches of my life, and then look to You to fix these pieces and make them stronger. I ask You to mend me so that I may bear the fruit of righteousness.

I cannot take credit for the times I do rise above such humbling circumstances. It is Your doing. I pray to be able to start trusting You from the beginning, to not require so much mending. I invite You to extend my branches to reach out in new ways. I stand by faith.

The Rubble of Old Ways

Like a city whose walls are broken down is a man who lacks self-control.

PROVERBS 25:28

I feel so vulnerable these days. My fortress of perceived togetherness and success has been destroyed. I step over the rubble that was once a supposedly good life and raise my hands to heaven. What now, Lord? What now?

I trust You to raise up what is truly an honorable, meaningful existence. Out of these ashes and the debris of broken dreams and an adjusted sense of happiness, I ask You to create something wonderful, something that reminds me what true love is.

Weak Are Made Strong

But we have this treasure in jars of clay to show that this all-surpassing power is from God and not from us.

2 CORINTHIANS 4:7

Anyone who knows the past problems in my life is amazed at how You continue to use me…a very broken, weak vessel. I am not whole in the way the world expects, but I am made whole, strong, and redeemable by Your grace. The cracks that other people see only increase the praise and credit I can offer You.

To those who wonder, I can say, "See this missing piece? See this shattered bit of pottery? My Potter is still able to fill me with His purpose and call me a worthy vessel." As I speak these words and pray this praise, I thank You, Lord, for calling me beautiful. I am a treasure that desires to be filled again and again.

A LITTLE UNDERSTANDING

On a Quest

So I turned my mind to understand, to investigate and to search out wisdom and the scheme of things and to understand the stupidity of wickedness and the madness of folly.

ECCLESIASTES 7:25

I am on a quest for knowledge, Lord. Something good that has come from my recent time of desperation and depletion is that I am hungry to understand and gather wisdom about how life works. Help me to see how my former ways might have complicated Your plan for my life. I do not want to dwell on these errors. You have forgiven them. But I do want to learn from my folly and my impatient days.

Give me a heart for what is true, holy wisdom. Guide my actions and thoughts so that I take this new knowledge and pull it into the way I live. I see this quest as an eternal thing. I no longer will be in a hurry to learn the lessons You have for me, Lord.

Learning to Ask

Ask and it will be given to you; seek and you will find; knock and the door will be opened to you.

MATTHEW 7:7

I am beginning to understand the whole asking thing. I come to You, prayerful and in need of so many things that I struggle to know where and how to begin. But my heart is leading the way, not my covetous, human spirit. I ask You today for comfort. There…I said it. I am hurt. I worry. I doubt those parts of me that used to seem like absolutes, like my faith, my hope in a future, and my ability to hear You.

I need You greatly, deeply, and now. I am standing at the door of my future and knocking. I no longer make demands while peeking through the keyhole. I wait till the door is wide open. I see Your compassion, and I fall to my knees. I am thankful You have opened up Your love to me.

9

Right Heart

When you ask, you do not receive, because you ask with wrong motives,
that you may spend what you get on your pleasures.

JAMES 4:3

I do not doubt that when I ask for things lately, I am asking with wrong motives. I am calling on Your power to transform my weak attempts or selfish inquiries into requests that are worthy of You. I am overwhelmed and have lost my ability to connect with most people around me. So when I come to You in that haze that defines me right now, I pray for Your grace.

You know my heart. Its motives are good. You see through all that is not me and reclaim for my future the real me…the me You created to have a right heart for You.

Encouraging Words

Stop doing wrong, learn to do right! Seek justice, encourage the oppressed.

ISAIAH 1:16-17

I keep telling myself to do better, to push through this moment in my life.
Will I recall ten years from now how hard this year was? I know I will remember the small kindnesses expressed by other people. My visual memories will be of the places I have visited and the faces that have appeared along my journey. I may not recall names, but I know that many impressions have been made on my heart.

Lord, encourage my spirit. When I am tempted to focus on my failings or missed opportunities, remind me that I am precious in Your sight.
I am learning to do right by myself and by You.

Figuring Out the Season

There is a time for everything,
and a season for every activity under heaven:
a time to be born and a time to die,
a time to plant and a time to uproot,
a time to kill and a time to heal,
a time to tear down and a time to build,
a time to weep and a time to laugh,
a time to mourn and a time to dance,
a time to scatter stones and a time to gather them,
a time to embrace and a time to refrain,
a time to search and a time to give up,
a time to keep and a time to throw away,
a time to tear and a time to mend,
a time to be silent and a time to speak,
a time to love and a time to hate,
a time for war and a time for peace.

ECCLESIASTES 3:1-8

Lord, I pray to understand what season I am in now. Reveal to me what this time is about in my life. Guide me toward the lessons I should take hold of. Stop me from making this time into a season that is not of You. Let this time of difficulty give way to a time of celebration and peace. I search my future for the new season that will surely come.

FRAGILE
and HOPEFUL

My Favorite Hiding Place

Rescue me from my enemies, O LORD, for I hide myself in you.

PSALM 143:9

If these current hurts can be my teachers, they offer me lessons about whom to trust and where to run. I cannot hide from life, though I have tried that during my weakest moments. But I can seek Your shelter when the most difficult enemies start to undermine my purpose. These enemies—fatigue, sorrow, doubt, fragility, stubbornness—seem insurmountable at times, until I can run to You.

Lord, You are my favorite hiding place. You offer a drink to cool me, a bed for rest, and protection against these threats to my life. Soon You will encourage me with words I need to hear. Then I will return to make my way through this circumstance, no longer weary, no longer fearful.

Walking the Valley

Even though I walk through the valley of the shadow of death, I will fear no evil, for you are with me; your rod and your staff, they comfort me.

PSALM 23:4

I am removed from those on the mountain. I look up and wave or nod to them along their journey. But I am here in the valley, Lord. This is where lush life grows, but for me it is a time of sorrow and uncertainty. I can only glance at those on higher plains once in a while, because my time here is so burdensome. Each step I take is my only focus.

But then up ahead I see You standing with Your rod and staff. You are waiting patiently and pointing out the secure places to step. I am almost there. Now we walk together, and You point out a mountain in the future that will be mine. Your promise to lead me out of the valley, Lord, is my only focus.

Colossians 3:15

13

14

Great Expectations

Watch and pray so that you will not fall into temptation.
The spirit is willing, but the body is weak.

MATTHEW 26:41

Oh, I am so willing, Lord. My spirit craves to do right. My heart beats so that I may grow to love You more. I pray for my life today and in the days ahead. I know there will be many times when I am tempted to quit the journey, stop caring, fade from my life.

Your love for me is my lifeline during these times. My spirit can cling to You and see the way through simple, everyday circumstances and the most difficult situations. It all feels hard right now, so I will not trust my first physical reaction. I will only trust the pull of my spirit toward Your presence.

Handle with Care

Turn to me and be gracious to me, for I am lonely and afflicted.

PSALM 25:16

Turn to me, Lord. Look at my face. See beyond the eyes, the lines, the signs of fatigue. See through to me. You understand what will raise me from this time. I cannot figure it out, and other people do not know what I need.

Turn to me, Lord. Be gracious to me. My loneliness haunts me. My pain is real. I have nobody to explain it to, figure it out with, who will fully understand. So I keep it all: the loneliness, the pain, the worry. It lies down with me, and even my dreams do not provide distance.

Turn to me, Lord. Let me rest my weary mind and body and spirit in Your presence while You watch over me.

A New Way

Knowing the Way Home

Show me your ways,
O LORD, teach me
your paths; guide me
in your truth and
teach me, for you are
God my Savior, and
my hope is in you all
day long.

PSALM 25:4-5

I have walked the roads back to myself and my old life so many times that I do it blindly, forgetting that You are taking me to a new place, along a new route. Forgive me for not rejoicing in this different journey. I had plans: people to see, things to do. I recognize that in hard times we learn great lessons that enrich our lives and our relationship with You. Even with this understanding, I am reluctant to follow at times.

So far, the scenery is not comforting. I must rely on You for everything: the map, the directions, safety along the way, and nourishment. No longer can I run to the places that used to be my refuge. This makes me anxious. Help me to place my hope in You, Lord. You do not guide me toward destruction, only toward resurrection from my old life. Give me faith to follow You home.

*B*linded by Trouble

Do not withhold your mercy from me, O Lord; may
your love and your truth always protect me. For troubles without
number surround me; my sins have overtaken me, and I cannot see.
They are more than the hairs of my head, and my heart fails within me.

PSALM 40:11-12

The darkness of my struggle covers my eyes and my heart.
I reach out my hands to feel my way through the mire. Troubles
more numerous than the sands of Your beaches and the hairs on
my head come at me, and in my blind state I have no response time.
Lord, protect me. Do not remove Your cover of mercy as
I relearn how to get through my days.

My heart beats slowly and without conviction. That perhaps is the
saddest part of my life right now. I am overwhelmed by my old
ways and old self. Release me from the patterns that hold
me hostage. Release me to Your mercy.

What Comes from Faith

But someone will say, "You have faith; I have deeds." Show me your faith without deeds, and I will show you my faith by what I do.

JAMES 2:18

Lord, thank You for my steadfast faith in earlier times. Oh, how You protected me from becoming too lazy in my belief. I let go of some of Your precepts when life went smoothly, but I have never removed myself from Your love and covering. I have never doubted that the goodness I tasted came from Your provision.

Now, as goodness seems foreign, I continue to express my life in the way of faith. My deeds are the result of a deeply rooted faith in You and Your strength and Your existence. Had I not developed traditions of prayer, forgiveness, and community, I would be left without a dwindling hope. Thank You. Thank You for inspiring a spiritual life with rich dimension. It holds me up in this moment.

YOUR SANCTUARY

Never Alone

Other people may come and go, leaving the life I know to go on to other things, but this is to be expected. Why, though, does this hurt me so? I take it personally that others are finding their foothold and stepping up or out, and You have called me to remain here alone, figuring it all out slowly and with much trepidation.

I know that I am not alone. I am never alone, for You are with me and You see where I stand. You see my sorrow and the loneliness that fills my days. I do not have a home to return to—not yet. But You prepare a place for me in this life and also in eternity. This is the future home I have to long for. This is the home that draws me back into the shelter of love and comfort.

Wisdom of the Widow

The loss of what is familiar to me leaves me feeling alone. God, You care for the most basic of my needs. I must trust You in the same way a widow does, as if my life depended on Your provision and mercy. This is truly a life of faith. When I felt strong and in control, I was losing sight of how to depend on You and Your help.

Night and day, I call out my needs to You and wait for them to be covered. The emptiness in me opens to the point of pain so that I can receive Your mercy. I am left alone with my thoughts and emotions, but I am never left alone in my need. Grant me the ability to firmly understand and praise You for this difference.

laced holly, garlands of pine
Winter is here, scenting the cold
Peace on Earth
goodwill to men, Let heaven and
laced holly, garlands of

Let love & faithfulness
never leave you;
bind them around
your neck,
Write them on
the tablet
of your heart.
Proverbs 3:3

NEW YORK
TIMES
COOKBOOK
Proverbs 30:6

22

Free in Our Slavery

Though we are slaves, our God has not deserted us in our bondage.
He has shown us kindness in the sight of the kings of Persia: He has
granted us new life to rebuild the house of our God and repair its ruins,
and he has given us a wall of protection in Judah and Jerusalem.

EZRA 9:9

My prison is becoming familiar to me. I fear I might become
accustomed to this sense of restriction and poverty and never return
to a life where I am totally free. God, be with me now and teach me
the lessons of freedom that You offered slaves and captives—those
who were mistreated, abused, and considered less than human.

The secret You offer is hope in the face of indifference, resurrection in
the face of death, and peace in the face of hatred. You give a new life to
those who seek Your face during their unfathomable moments in the
pit of despair. You protect the most important part of me, Lord. You
know it is my soul, my spirit that must rise above these circumstances.
Through my spirit, I will forever be free.

*M*odel Behavior

Whatever you have learned or received or heard from me, or seen in me—put it into practice. And the God of peace will be with you.

PHILIPPIANS 4:9

During this time, I have spent moments reflecting on the blessing of those people who model a strong faith. I thank You for the gifts of friends, family members, and strangers who have shown me aspects of Your character. I draw on this heritage when I need to make decisions.

There are days when I am functioning on autopilot. God, I want to surrender my actions to Your will. I want to step out with a strong faith. When I do not know what to do, I will rely on what I have learned, received, and heard from those who have walked before me.

*A*ction

But Jesus immediately said to them: "Take courage! It is I. Don't be afraid." "Lord, if it's you," Peter replied, "tell me to come to you on the water." "Come," he said. Then Peter got down out of the boat, walked on the water and came toward Jesus.

MATTHEW 14:27-29

When You call us into action, Lord, it is for our own good. It is a way of moving us forward and toward a future. Because I am so weary, I long to sit. I fantasize about falling into a deep slumber and waking up once this struggle is over. But, Lord, You waken me to the wonder of trusting You.

Help me recognize Your face and Your voice as You call me to take action. What should I do, Lord? Ask it of me, and give me the strength…and the faith…to follow through.

The

the pace, and the air is softly scented

my garden wall. A drive to the ocean,

berries and golden gentle scented climb to th

The songbirds praise their creator

golden sunlight. Summertime has

birds praise their creator

25

God Appears

Let us acknowledge the LORD; let us press on to acknowledge him.
As surely as the sun rises, he will appear; he will come to us like the winter rains,
like the spring rains that water the earth.

HOSEA 6:3

I am not aware of much these days. I pray to be perceptive of how You move
through me and around me. I need these signs of Your activity in my life. Much
escapes my attention. I am slow to catch what people are saying to me.
It is only by Your grace that I get through the days.

While in this time of hibernation, I pray to be awakened to Your touch. May I notice it
in the rising sun and the life-giving rains. These are not only symbols of hope, but are
also evidence of Your active presence. This is a truth I so desperately need to hold on to.

Know When to Stand Firm

Therefore, my dear brothers, stand firm. Let nothing move you. Always give yourselves fully
to the work of the Lord, because you know that your labor in the Lord is not in vain.

1 CORINTHIANS 15:58

I am making slow but sure progress toward my goals. I sense Your leading and
have received wise counsel from people of faith. I am giving myself over to the work
You have placed in front of me, and I am thankful for it. I realize that there are times
You ask me to not move. You require me to be still and stand firm.

Having an unmoving faith means I must lean against the rock of Your strength.
I cling to it and know the form of its power so well. My ideas change and my opinions
vary, but I do not move from my life's foundation.

27

Healing

The Process

> Blessed are those
> who mourn, for they
> will be comforted.
>
> MATTHEW 5:4

I am used to taking aspirin when my head aches. I drink fizzy beverages when my stomach hurts. But when my heart aches and my life is broken, I must face the spiritual process for healing. I must release myself to mourning. Lord, I can only do this because You are my Foundation.

I give myself over to Your comfort. Giving way to the flood of sorrow is not easy for me, Lord. I like to stay in control. You know all that needs healing in my life. Reach down and inspire my healing to begin.

Looking Ahead

> I know that my
> Redeemer lives, and
> that in the end he will
> stand upon the earth.
>
> JOB 19:25

When I want explanations for my circumstances or easy fixes for my ailing life, I know that I am requesting unnecessary things. You do not call me to "get" everything about my troubles. You do call me to trust You. It is not with reprimands or rules that You require this of me. It is through Your love.

I cannot be certain how this time will play out. I do not know the answers that will come my way, or if only more questions will fill my mind. The vision of healing I hope for might not come to pass. You might offer something completely different for my life.

What I do know is that, at the very end, I will experience healing as I run to You—my Redeemer.

I Will

Heal me, O Lord, and I will be healed; save me and I will be saved,
for you are the one I praise.

JEREMIAH 17:14

I will ask to be healed, and I will be healed. I will ask to be saved, and I will be saved. You are the One I come to in my distress or frustration, because You are with me in my times of fulfillment and contentment. So I know You are with me now. Praising what You are doing in my life feels awkward at times, because it seems so far from a hopeful situation. Yet, I praise You honestly and with belief that I am precious to You.

I will muster up the courage to ask, Lord. And I will hear Your response of acceptance, love, and comfort.

$\mathcal{B}$ecause It Is Done

He said to me: "It is done. I am the Alpha and the Omega,
the Beginning and the End. To him who is thirsty I will give to drink
without cost from the spring of the water of life."

REVELATION 21:6

You started and finished all that needs to be done,
for now and for all time. There is nothing I need to accomplish that
will change or secure that. That is not my job nor the purpose You
have given to me. I am to be in covenant with You, seeking Your
presence and following in Your way so that I honor, accept,
and give glory to the Alpha and the Omega.

Because You have done all that is required, You offer refreshment with
the water of life. There is no need to explain my thirst, because You
know all that I experience. And as I drink to fill my need,
I know there is no cost because You already paid it.

BEYOND EXCUSES

Forgive

Lately, I have been blaming other people for my misery. People not even involved in my struggles are suddenly in my way or the cause of trouble. I feel frustrated by those who go about life without problems right now. I realize I cannot see what they struggle with, but in my desire to find reasons for my hurt, I want to blame other people.

Lord, where there are real grievances, please help me forgive the person and to see beyond the situation. May I never use another person as a reason to not follow Your lead.

Putting the Past to Rest

I flip through my history as though I am looking at a photo album of past mistakes. I take the images out, one by one, and I scrutinize everything about the moment. *What was I thinking? How could I? How was I to know? I was so stupid. I should never have.* It is an endless cycle of guilt, such a waste of energy.

I pray to forget what is behind me so that I can press on toward the goal. You have a purpose for my life. When I spend my time reflecting on the past, I am avoiding the future. Do not let me waste another day focused on regrets.

Send Me

Then I heard the voice of the Lord saying, "Whom shall I send?
And who will go for us?" And I said, "Here am I. Send me!"

ISAIAH 6:8

No more hiding—I have tried that in the past, and my problems still
find me. When will I learn that it is better to stand up at the beginning
and ask You to send me out into my future, Your will, and my life? I
want to have the courage to say, "Send me" to You, Lord. When You
are seeking hearts that long to abide by Your Word and to trust Your
guidance, I want to be counted faithful.

I could hide forever. I could make up reasons why
I do not want to move forward and trust Your will,
but no more. Send me, Lord. Here I am.

Belief

Never Failing

You know with all your heart and soul that not one of all the good promises the Lord your God gave you has failed. Every promise has been fulfilled; not one has failed.

JOSHUA 23:14

I can read off a list of mistakes, broken promises, and unfulfilled expectations, but this list only reflects my own side of our relationship, Lord. I see Your faithfulness in every turn of my life. I struggle to remember that during my darker days or times like now, when I feel I am juggling too many responsibilities and everyone else is letting me down.

So when I am ready to complain that there is nowhere to turn, that there is nothing to believe in anymore, remind me, Lord, that You are a God who keeps His Word…to me, to my life, to this faith journey I am on.

One More Time

I have asked to do this a few times in my past, but I am most certain that this time is the most crucial to my faith, Lord. Please, can I look at the holes in Your hands one more time? Can I approach You as Thomas did, filled with doubt and questions and uncertainty? It is not so much that I am on a quest for proof. I just need assurance. I need You to calm me once again with Your peace.

And I need You to call me on this behavior and say, "Stop doubting and believe." I am ready to get back to all that You have for me in this life, Lord. But can I look, just one more time?

Though the doors were locked, Jesus came and stood among them and said, "Peace be with you!" Then he said to Thomas, "Put your finger here; see my hands. Reach out your hand and put it into my side. Stop doubting and believe." Thomas said to him, "My Lord and my God!"

JOHN 20:26-28

Colossians 3:16

38

Just As I Believe

Then Jesus said to the centurion, "Go! It will be done just as you believed it would."
And his servant was healed at that very hour.

MATTHEW 8:13

Lord, You give me belief, and then honor that belief with miracles every day. It is only when I waver, when I start relying on myself or other people too much that Your touch begins to fade. Our relationship involves both of us, and I do not always hold up my part.

Today I need You so badly. I come to You with deep, abiding faith.
I am in my last hour of strength for this journey, Lord. I have waited too long to give myself over to disbelief. You take my hand and lead me to a higher place where hope rushes about me and I am revived.

Morning 'Til Night

Show me your ways, O LORD, teach me your paths; guide me in your truth and teach me,
for you are God my Savior, and my hope is in you all day long.

PSALM 25:4-5

I awaken to Your mercies, Lord. I know that I do not get out of bed and go to work without the sustaining power of Your love. While my mind spins with frustrations and possible worst-case scenarios for my life, You calm my emotions and let me focus on the job before me. You even help me see the needs of other people in the midst of my own need.

I come home feeling I have actually accomplished something—an amazing feeling that curbs my feelings of going nowhere in my time of trial. Some nights I cannot sleep, yet even then You are there to comfort me and teach me patience. Each day, morning 'til night, is such a gift when I give it over to You, Lord.

JOY

Because of Hope

*Be joyful in hope,
patient in affliction,
faithful in prayer.
Share with God's people
who are in need.
Practice hospitality.*

ROMANS 12:12-13

Because my faith tells me that tomorrow will be different, I have hope. Because I have this hope in my heart, I have joy. My difficulties are not fading, nor are they being removed from my responsibilities right now, but I have joy.

When I feel I have nothing to give, You call me to extend Your love to other people, and in that act of obedience I find joy. How You are able to lift my spirit out of the depths of despair, Lord, is the greatest mystery and delight of my faith. Thank You, Lord.

Crossing Over

*Restore to me the joy
of your salvation and
grant me a willing
spirit, to sustain me.*

PSALM 51:12

I have been a reluctant child of Yours lately. I am dragging my feet and my spirit right along with 'em. God, I really want to have a willing spirit. I want to draw from Your well of salvation and sip of Your mercy and joy. I want to experience this renewal now. I just need help crossing over from this place of apathy to the place of belief.

Help me to watch for Your provision. Turn my feet toward Your heart. I want to walk to You, crawl to You—whatever it takes to cross over that line I have created that separates me from Your joy.

Way to Joy

Finally, brothers, whatever is true, whatever is noble, whatever is right, whatever is pure, whatever is lovely, whatever is admirable—if anything is excellent or praiseworthy—think about such things.

PHILIPPIANS 4:8

I know the way to joy. I watch other people about me also go through their struggles, and they do not know that the way of joy exists, let alone how to get there. You give me what I need to persevere and receive the joy of eternity. I might want to gather troubles, trip over them, shove them aside, and bring them out again, but You tell me to let go of such things and turn my attention to whatever is true, noble, right, pure, lovely, admirable, excellent, and praiseworthy.

Just repeating that list, Lord, reminds me of the goodness in my life and all around me. Through the rubble of destruction, Lord, Your words and Your truth carve out the way to joy.

Something About Today

This day is sacred to our LORD.
Do not grieve, for the joy of the Lord is your strength.

NEHEMIAH 8:10

I start out the day with steps that are heavy with grief.
I feel the pressure of life on my shoulders and begin to cave toward
the sidewalk. My countenance is drawn and expressionless. I see how
other people respond to me and am taken aback by the reflection of
my sadness in their eyes. Then, out of nowhere and straight from Your
hand, a single perfect leaf rushes past my line of vision. I watch it float,
taking its time. It does not rush to the ground with
the weight of burdens.

It is as if I can see Your hand cradling this symbol of a new season.
You let it glide in the sky, and then You gently guide it to safety. The
wind on my back becomes Your gentle hand, and I know that today
is sacred. It is a day in which my journey is guided to safety by Your
strength and will. I give myself over to this with great relief.

Paying Attention

The Best Part

Lord, is the best part of me showing right now? Is my focus so much on my problems that I do not allow my godly character to make an appearance? I worry that my complaining has become my only communication, that my sighs and tears have become the only evidence that I am alive.

May my hope in You be the force which moves me to interact with people. May my upright life and character be honorable and evident in all that I do and say. Your hope is the best part of me and of this time in my life. May it shine.

Chitchat

I overdid it, Lord. Once my mouth opened up, it was useless. Everything in me poured out: the hurt, the questions, the doubting, the anger. I was not paying attention to the person I was talking to, and I ignored this individual's need for consolation, not commiseration. I know what this is like. I have come to You so many times after someone has done the same to me.

"This is my heart, be careful with it." This is what we require of one another, yet we are foolish. We turn the situation into a stage for our woeful performance. I pray to become wise in such matters, Lord.

I thought I would
write you a letter with my
new letter paper I got for
my birth... Quote Yourselves to pray...
and I go... being ... and thank...
handkerch... and pray ... for us
a box of ... too ... that ... God may ...
candy and... open ... a door for
... our ... message ...
... so that ... we may proclaim ...
... the ... of ... kind
... Christ ... which ... is
... am in Jesus. ...

Miss Ada Hunter
Dinuba
Cal.

P E A C E

Dear Aunt,
Wishing you
many happy
birthday
from all,

... all send you kisses
Your son
Jimmie Moreng

Dear Nellie
Thanks for T. C. J. B ...
am sorry you have
grown so plain ...

No Substitute

An honest answer is like a kiss on the lips.

PROVERBS 24:26

Meaningful...full of promise...trusting...vulnerable...
appreciated...remembered. Honesty is such a powerful way to express
love to another person...Your love. It becomes a kiss on the lips to
someone in need of affection and tenderness.

When I am tempted to offer someone an answer that
is less than truthful about my circumstances, Lord, help me to see how
my honesty in that moment could be a gift for myself and the other
person. Let me release my pride and be willing to share the hard stuff
when I feel led. Just when I want to call my hardship a jagged
rock, an open wound, You are ready to turn it
into a beautiful gem, a sweet kiss.

Let the morning bring
me word of your unfailing love,
for I have put my trust in you.
Show me the way I should go,
for to you I lift up my soul.

PSALM 143:8

fall to the ground apart from the will of
And even the hairs of your head are all numbered
sold for a penny? Yet not one of them will
ground apart from the will of your Father. And even